A special gift for

_____

Essence of Wisdom for Parents

Ted LaFemina

ESSENCE OF WISDOM FOR PARENTS
© 2009, 2012 Ted LaFemina

Printed in the United States of America
ALL RIGHTS RESERVED

No part of this publication may be reproduced, stored in a retrieval system, or transmitted, in any form or by any means – mechanical, electronic, photocopying, recording, or otherwise – without prior written permission.

Published by Pressed Thoughts LLC
www.pressedthoughts.com

ISBN 978-0-9850102-1-8

Dedication

Dedicated to all the men and women who take their role as parents both seriously and joyously, and to the grandparents, family, and friends that support them.

With special thanks to my amazing wife and children, to my mother and father who both taught me how to love in different ways, to my uncle Paul who took me aside as soon as he heard I was going to be a father and told me to just love my children, and to all my family & friends who shared their own wisdom with me.

Also special thanks to the Reverend Tim, Pastor Lew, Lisa, Ron, Steve, James, Trish, Dr. Vince, Joe, and Teddy for taking the time to review this book and provide invaluable feedback.

Introduction

Compiled within these pages is an eclectic collection of both serious and light-hearted wisdom gathered from many sources and many people. Some of this wisdom is thousands of years old and has been handed down for generations. Some is new and relevant to the modern world we live in. None is universally accepted.

The hope of the author is that this book will start some conversations. Conversations between you and your spouse, between you and some close friends, and perhaps between you and your parents. If you're lucky, you'll be able to maintain these conversations throughout your parenting process. You may find that your views on some of the topics evolve over time. You may also find that these conversations trigger new thoughts and ideas that will help you to grow as a parent, or handle some of the more difficult situations you'll surely face.

And finally, you may find that you'll be prepared to offer some comfort to other parents as they struggle with their own issues by sharing some of the wisdom contained on these pages, and some you have developed on your own. This process can help build close friendships and a community to surround your family.

TABLE OF CONTENTS

Wisdom for New Parents.............1

Wisdom for All Parents..............41

Wisdom for Parents of Teens..113

Wisdom for Marriage 135

Wisdom for New Parents

Wisdom for New Parents

Listen to the advice of others but don't treat it as gospel. You'll have to navigate your own path.

Husband

When you go to pick your wife and baby up from the hospital for the first time, bring her a little gift and some good food.

The best indication that you *are* a great parent is the fact that you have a strong *desire* to be a great parent.

All parents are imperfect, all kids are different, and there is no single right way of being a parent.

A great parent is one who does the best that they can, with love, and always has the desire (if not the energy) to continue being that great parent.

Be ready to set aside any preconceived notions of what you can accomplish once your baby has arrived and learn to just go with the flow.

You will be too tired to do all of it - or even most of it.

Wisdom for New Parents

Babies need "skin time." So does your spouse.

If your newborn infant doesn't latch on when you are trying to feed it, it doesn't mean that they don't love you. They will figure it out. (Try the football hold if you haven't already.)

The hormone surge after birth, lack of sleep, and a crying baby can make your emotions race. Don't let the emotions get the best of you; just relax and enjoy this amazing experience. If it's a challenge, know that things will settle down in time. If it gets too overwhelming, talk to your doctor about it.

A woman's view of her body can change after delivering and nursing her first baby. This can be a difficult adjustment for both husband and wife.

In some ways, this time is really when your marriage begins.

Make sure you have an appropriate car seat before your baby is born.

Make sure that you know how to install it properly in your car.

Keep your kids in car seats and booster seats until it is safe for them to get out — not simply when it is legal. If you ever flip your car, you will be glad you did.

Infants and babies are not used to silence. They like background noise.

Never wake up a sleeping baby to feed it.

Wisdom for New Parents

Read *On Becoming Baby-Wise* — especially the part about getting the baby on schedule and about teaching the baby to settle down on their own.

Read *What to expect when you're Expecting*, and *What to Expect, the Toddler years*.

Essence of Wisdom for Parents

Don't take articles in parenting magazines too seriously. If you read this stuff too much, you will stress yourself out trying to "get everything right." Kids are really pretty durable.

Trust your instincts, and trust yourself. It's all on-the-job training and you're not going to do it all perfectly all the time. Don't be so hard on yourself.

Move your baby out of your bedroom when they are still an infant and don't let them jump into your bed or you will never get them out.

Wisdom for New Parents

Sing to your babies – it lightens the heart.

Realize that kids will act their age. Know what this means.

When you tell your kid, "No," follow through. Don't make threats you can't back up. If you tell your child to come to you, and they don't, go get them! Don't negotiate with them or beg them to listen to you. If you do, they will grow up to be more defiant and harder to deal with. When they become teenagers, it will be impossible.

Don't buy too much stuff. Take advantage of hand-me-downs. Beware that clothing and toys accumulate exponentially, so don't buy more than you absolutely need. They can get by with comfy play clothes until they go to school.

If you can afford for mom to stay home – do it! Once you weigh in child care, the cost of eating fast food nightly during the week and the toys you buy out of guilt for not being involved with your child's life, its tough to save any real money anyway. You may find that working is not a big financial benefit.

Generally, children are better learners, better behaved, better disciplined, and better people when raised by a parent. These characteristics can save lots of pain when they are in high school, and even in their adult years.

Teach your toddler pre-school things.

Avoid talking to your child with baby talk. Regular talk will help them learn.

Disgusting is an adult concept.

Just get used to it.

Most kids really only need a bath once per week – but it can be great quality time if you want it to be part of your routine.

Kids have a very short attention span. Learn to use this if they are ever hurt or if you need to remove a toy.

Colorful band-aids are really cool and relatively cheap.

Beanbags left in the freezer have amazing healing properties for bumps and bruises: even if they don't really help the bump or bruise.

Have more than one child so that they have a playmate, so that they learn to fight and forget, and so that they can take turns caring for you when you are old.

Parenting gets easier when the younger children get big enough to fight back with the older children.

Kids learn about families and what a mom is by being with them. This is much more important than preschool or even kindergarten. They can always learn how to paste later.

Attend retirement parties and going away lunches at your office. Make a note of how disinterested many of the guests are and how quickly the office can get along without the person leaving.

Understand that no job that you can do will have more impact in the world than the job of raising your child.

Treat this job with the respect and priority that it deserves.

Kids bite through at least the age of four.

Age and amputation are the only successful means for stopping a kid from sucking their thumb.

Trying to stop them with hot-sauce, socks over their hands, or other tricks only teaches them how to resist their parents and put up with your discipline.

Just relax. It will stop before high school.

Kids love pure cane sugar. If you go to a coffee shop, make sure you get them a sugar packet and a stir-stick that they can use to dip and lick.

(Open the sugar packets for your children.)

Lookup tuition rates of the local university and find out what the average annual tuition increases are. Then work out a savings plan. A financial planner can help with this.

Brace yourself.

Find a good babysitter now! You will need to set up regular date nights with your spouse. It's OK if the date is at Wal-Mart®.

Keep a notebook for your kids and write down the cute things they do and say. It's easy for these memories to get lost in time.

Have plenty of tickle sessions on the bed with your child, but make sure that you let them breath between tickles.

Wisdom for New Parents

Wisdom for All Parents

Parenting books are great, but parents should understand that most of these books are for kids who fall within the parameters of *average*. Parents need to understand that their kid might not be average. They have to listen to their own gut when their kid doesn't do what the book says they should, and take whatever steps they think appropriate for their child.

Micromanage your kid's homework and schoolwork.

Wisdom for All Parents

Sign your kids up for music when they are in school so that they learn to play an instrument.

Don't spoil your kids.

Chores are a natural part of being in a family.

Allowance can get expensive, especially with multiple kids. Be careful what precedents you set.

Allowances do help to teach your kids money management which is an important, but not always natural, skill.

A well-adjusted family home will never look perfect. Do keep the filth down and the kitchen clean, but be prepared to deal with some level of clutter. Otherwise, you will put unnecessary stress on the rest of your family.

Cleaning your house before guests arrive is a way to honor them, but pretending to be someone you are not will always dampen the quality of a relationship.

A good goal in life is to develop the kind of friends that will be glad to come over and help you clean up before guests arrive.

Raising children involves an endless succession of deadly risks. If your child dies accidentally, don't blame yourself or your spouse but rather provide mutual comfort to each other.

All people are hardwired with an inherent risk threshold; it is likely that yours is different from that of your spouse. Have respect for your spouse's risk tolerance level and do not assume that yours is always right.

Most of life's greatest experiences have some risk associated with it and children only thrive when they take some level of risk. On the other hand, taking an unnecessary risk is foolish.

Work with your spouse on these decisions.

When going to the emergency room, bring magazines, kids books, snacks, and snack money. You will be there a while.

Worry can no more change the future than regret can change the past.

If you are confronted with a true tragedy in your life, then do not turn to your children to be your counselors, but do not hide your pain or tears from them either.

It can be more difficult for a child to deal with these situations if they do not think that their parents have emotions similar to what they are experiencing.

Real men and women cry.

Hug and kiss your spouse lovingly in front of your kids.

Wisdom for All Parents

Always hug and kiss your kids and tuck them in at night (even through high school).

Young kids are tactilely stimulated not visually or intellectually stimulated, at least through elementary school. If they can't touch it, then it's boring.

Play classical music for your kids.

Quality time is a myth.
Quantity time is the only thing that matters.

Every once in a while, get down on the floor and hang out with your kids on their level.

Kids need self-directed time and activities.

Be prepared for surprises and do your best to deal with them when they happen.

Parenthood is a lifelong commitment that is immeasurably cruel to break.

Seek to grow in your faith with God and do this in front of your children so that they can learn what being a Christian really means.

It's not possible to truly love others until you can love yourself.

So that you can properly love your kids, live your life in a manner that allows you to love yourself and be proud of yourself — for some, this may be a process.

Forgive yourself of anything in the past that you're not proud of and focus on the future.

Get mentoring from older couples at church. Get to know them and occasionally ask for tips on marriage and child rearing.

Children are born as uncivilized savages and it is your responsibility to spend the first twenty years of their life changing this fact.

Make sure that your child knows that you are the boss. Do this at all costs as if your child's life depends upon it — because it does.

Some kids are strong-willed children and some are not. Do not look down on other parents if they have one and you do not. It only means that you haven't had more kids yet. Your turn may come.

Children listen to your whispers, more carefully then they do your shouting.

Kids like routine. They also like boring foods like macaroni and cheese, hotdogs (without condiments), and bologna.

At family gatherings, have plenty of finger food out for the younger kids to grab as they run around. Don't expect young younger children to sit down like adults and stay still for the meal portion of the day. This is stressful on them and stressful on you.

Kids remember every promise, even ones they consider implied promises.

Have family game nights. Be inclusive with your children's friends.

Have dinner together as a family.

Taking the time to listen to your children is an excellent way to show love. It will build a foundation that will help in their teenage years.

Have patience. Learn to count to ten.

Remember to take care of yourself occasionally so that you have the energy to continue serving the family.

Don't let your kids watch TV, especially when they are under age four. Read up and study the effects of TV. It is very bad.

Most *family* shows, on *family* networks that target young kids actually teach kids to be disrespectful to parents. They are not family friendly.

If you read books yourself and don't let your kids watch TV, then they will learn to enjoy reading books.

Read to your children.

Essence of Wisdom for Parents

Always! Always! be an advocate for your kid. The doctor doesn't always know best. Neither do the grandparents, neighbors, etc. If you think it's important, or that there's something wrong with your child, don't let anyone dissuade you from going to a specialist, getting tests done, having the kid checked out, or whatever it takes to get them the help they need.

Advocate for your child vigorously in school if your child has special needs.

Rally the support of teachers if you can. The system will be against you.

Limit electronic and computer game time and monitor what your children are playing. Violent and inappropriate games are bad for them.

Sign your kids up for sports and then go to all their games (both parents) and enjoy them!

Let them hear you yell *Go! Go!* every once in a while.

Never let them hear you treat coaches, referees, umpires, other parents, or other players with disrespect.

Every once in a while, embarrass your kids with your affection.

Feed your kids a healthy diet – give them soda and corn syrup drinks in extreme moderation.

If you are near a pool or a pond and you don't hear your child, it is because they are drowning.

When outside, always make sure you can run to your child faster than they can run to the street.

If your children are playing and things get quiet, go check on them.

Enjoy your kids now. They won't stay at this age very long. However, you still have to be a parent.

Both parents should take turns going on field trips. It shows your kids you care about them, and it gives you a chance to see that your child is normal.

Wisdom for All Parents

If you are watching your kids play and they fall, keep a straight face. If you do, they will get back up and keep playing. If you flinch, they will start balling.

Be consistent: it's unfair to them if you are not.

Wisdom for All Parents

Teach your kids that life isn't fair.

Support your spouse's handling of your child's discipline in front of them. Settle disagreements in private. Do not let your kids play you.

It's OK for your kids to see you and your spouse have an argument every once in a while as long as it's a healthy argument. It teaches your kids how to have a disagreement while at the same time listening and showing respect for each other. It also shows them that it's important to stand up for what's right, to back down when your wrong, and to expand your view of issues when someone provides you a new way to look at them.

Spanking is extremely appropriate sometimes. It's best if it comes immediately following the offense. Child abuse is *never* appropriate.

If sending your kids to the corner works, then one minute per year of age will be about right. Ask them why they were punished when they come out so they learn. Do not be surprised when they occasionally forget what they did.

Learn to criticize behaviors, not people. This will set a good example for your kids.

Never let your kids hear you blaming other people for your own choices.

Listen to each word that comes out of your month for the next 30 days, and then note the percentage of those words that are encouraging.

Repeat as necessary.

Wisdom for All Parents

There are three major forms of profanity: those related to bodily functions, those related to intimate relations, and those related to racial and ethnic slurs.

Decide which of these you would be proud to hear your child use, and then keep talking that way.

If you have a gun in the house, then know that it is a near certainty that your child and one of their friends will find it and play with it eventually.

Follow all the gun safety best practices.

Teach your children to have a strong work ethic and to seek, rather than fear, challenging opportunities.

Taking on and accomplishing challenging tasks causes great personal growth and is one of the most rewarding things to do in life.

Generally, people are most happy when in the process of achieving a worthwhile goal.

Have a one-on-one date with each of your children at least once a year.

Breakfast on their birthday works.

Read, study, understand, and contemplate everything the Bible says about raising children and about marriage. Get a study Bible in a translation that is readable to you. Learn to use the footnotes and cross-reference systems.

Recognize that God gave us children so that we can understand His relationship with us and that He gave us marriage so that we can understand our relationship with Jesus and the Holy Spirit.

Use this understanding to build up a base of wisdom for dealing with parenting and marriage issues *before* you have issues that need to be dealt with. If you wait, it may be too late.

Give your child your blessing.

Tell your kids you love them and are proud of them. Not for what they do, but for who they are. Make sure that you hug your kids and occasionally give them a shoulder squeeze

Kids need to *hear* it, and they need to *feel* it. It's not sufficient for them to just "know" that they are loved.

Fathers are notoriously deficient in these things.

Love your child. If you love your child, all other things will work out.

Wisdom for Parents of Teens

Recognize that the human brain is incapable of making risk based decisions until the age 25. Prior to 25, the emotional center of the brain makes these decisions. (This is supported by NIH research — and most parents with kids under 25.)

Alter your approach to parenting when your children become teens.

Transition from directing to steering.

When kids become teens, their awareness of the time matures. Share family plans and calendar events with them.

Encourage your high schooler to be involved in high school teams and clubs and find a way to get involved yourself so that you get to know other parents and can keep tabs on what is really going on.

Build a social circle for yourself that will stay with you once your kids grow up and leave. You can do this by working to deepen the relationships you make through school support activities.

Once your children leave the nest, it can get very lonely and depressing if you have neglected this.

In critical situations, a strong and very natural tendency for teens is to give more weight to the opinion of their friends than to the potential consequences of their decisions.

Make sure that they understand this natural tendency and the importance of overriding it.

Continually work to grow your sense of compassion for all those around you and teach your kids to do the same – especially as they get older.

Do not negotiate with teens, but do listen to them and then explain your decision making process.

Do not say "No" automatically to every request.

Demanding respect rarely works.

Giving respect rarely fails.

The emotional parts of the brain grow more rapidly during the teenage years than the parts of the brain that moderate those emotions.

Expect to see wide swings in anger, excitement, frustration, depression, and indignation.

Do not respond to these in kind, but rather with patience, forgiveness, and empathy.

Copernicus was wrong. The world actually revolves around teenage girls.

Teach your kids to never let fear stop them from joining a conversation, doing something good, or standing up to evil.

Also teach them to be inviters.

A great conversation with your teen consists of you sharing what they need to know, and them muttering *I already know that — Can I leave now?*

Do not neglect these conversations.

If your teen initiates a conversation with you then bite your tongue and just listen. If you are too quick to share your good advice or judgment, they will stop talking to you.

Honest conversation from your teen is a privilege, not a right.

Do not automatically trust the moral judgment and common sense of the parents of your teen's friends.

Explain to your teens that their behavior sets a powerful example for their friends — whether the behavior is good or bad.

The smarter, friendlier, or more athletic your teen is, the greater their responsibility to set a good example.

Do not try to live out your unrealized dreams through your children, but rather help and encourage them to find and live out their own ambitions.

As your teens grow older, teach them about real world finances.

Teach your kids how to cook and do laundry. It doesn't hurt to make these part of their regular chores.

If your child starts to date, explain to them the need to tread lightly on the heart of their partner, especially during a painful breakup.

A mother and father's goal is to raise their children and then set them free. Prepare them for the second step of this process.

It's a good idea to prepare yourselves as well.

Wisdom for Marriage

—

Being good parents implies having a good marriage. Good marriages are not automatic.

Husband

Success is measured by how well you meet your responsibilities, by the degree that you are able to self-actualize, and by the level at which you help others to do the same. The first of these is the most important, the second the least important. As a husband you have many responsibilities to your wife: you must provide financial and emotional security, you must provide spiritual leadership and support, and you must provide companionship and love. Work on these things for the rest of your life.

Make sure that your self-image is derived from your understanding that God created you as a unique, special human being that He loves. Do not allow yourself to derive your self-image from your career, your possessions, your appearance, or from what others may think of you.

Husband

Build your wife's self-image, especially if she is a stay-at-home mom that has no other support for her sense of value. If you don't, then her quality of life will slowly diminish and so will yours.

Wife

Build your man's self-image and sense of manhood. Trust him.

Your spouse will be with you long after your children have left home. Do not put your children first and do not neglect your marriage.

Husband

When you get home from work after dealing with complex business problems, your wife will be at the door waiting to chat with you about diaper problems and how much dust is under the refrigerator. Remember that the socialization with your wife is way more important than your business problems. Listen to her and enjoy the blessing of having that time. There is no guarantee that you will have the same opportunity again.

Wife

When your husband gets home from work, he may want to sit in a hole for a while. Don't worry or anguish about this. Men are just wired this way.

Wife

Allow your husband to be a man.

Set goals mutually but support your husband in the path toward achievement.

Bad marriages happen slowly. Never stop taking the time to be aware of, and appreciate, the unique qualities in your partner for life.

Never allow yourself to drift into *what-if* thoughts about your life if you chose not to marry or if you chose to marry someone else. All paths in life can be a challenge.

The true joy in life is meeting the challenge with renewed love, caring, and compassion.

Husband

Read books that explain women and marriage. Get recommendations for these books at church.

Wife

Read books that explain men and marriage. Get recommendations for these books at church.

Divorce is always due to selfishness.

Divorce is only an option in the case of abuse and unfaithfulness.

Husband

Lustfully looking at other women is adultery. It does cause pain and is wrong.

Look good for your spouse, but learn to dress modestly in front of others.

Revealing or provocative dress is usually effective and can lead to unhealthy situations.

If husbands and wives understood the pain inflicted on them and on their children from divorce they would be more diligent about preventing the things that lead to it.

The first sign of spousal abuse is when your spouse tries to control your money, or isolate you from your friends or family. Recognize your natural inclination to fool yourself and seek professional counseling immediately if this happens to you.

If you enjoy drinking, then periodically ask your spouse if they think the drinking is a problem. If they answer *yes*, then you have, by definition, a drinking problem and should stop.

A good rule of thumb for an adult with responsibilities is that any more than 1-2 drinks a week is a problem and may indicate that you are having challenges in life that you don't know how to deal with.

Men's and women's small groups in church are a good starting place to get help.

If your spouse is abusive, (physically, verbally, or emotionally), or if you think your spouse would not be a good parent, then if you do not yet have children: don't. If you already have children you have a responsibility to protect them. You may be willing to live with abuse, but children should not.

Love is a verb. It is something you do, not a feeling you have.

Husband

Adore your wife.

Learn the unique ways in which your spouse expresses their love. This may be through words, through service, through gift giving, through touch, and through time. Return this type of love to them.

Exhaustion and frustration are not licenses to speak rudely or in anger.

Husband

Do not perpetuate the dreams and desires of a single man in your mind. Build dreams with your wife instead and constantly revel in the blessing God has given you by bringing her into your life.

Tip: If it has an engine in it, and is really fast, it's probably a single man's desire.

Husband

The things that can be most hurtful to your wife and therefore most affect your own happiness are your thoughts, followed by your words, followed by your actions. Your actions being far behind your words and thoughts.

Husband

Your wife will be able to most easily forgive your actions, followed by your words and, being by far the most difficult: your thoughts.

Learn instantaneous forgiveness.

Anger serves as an anesthetic for emotional pain usually caused by misguided expectations. Don't hold onto anger just to numb your pain — it is destructive to yourself and your relationships.

Learn how to deal with emotional pain in constructive ways.

Never grow into the habit of talking past your spouse.

When you have information to share, give your spouse time to switch mental contexts and make sure that they are engaged in the conversation.

In any conversation, make the effort to insure that you both understand what each other are saying.

When things are not going well, *never* seek comfort and companionship with a friend of the opposite sex.

Instead seek council from a wise friend who is interested in supporting your relationship, not supporting your complaining.

Husband

A husband is never happier than his wife for any extended period of time.

Husband

A man's home is where he sleeps and eats. A woman's home is an extension of herself. Remember this when she wants help cleaning and decorating it.

Husband

It's your house too. Help keep it clean, every time you walk through a room.

Wife

Your husband's brain is incapable of perceiving clutter and dirt. It also isn't very good at finding things in the pantry.

Do something a little extra for your spouse every once in a while. Don't get in the habit of doing the minimum necessary to be a good partner.

Take time to notice and appreciate all the things your spouse does for you, even if they do it every day.

Don't refrain from difficult conversations with your spouse. If you do, it can lead you to an attitude of passive aggression and sarcasm as a means of expressing your dissatisfaction.

This is unfair and takes all the joy out of a relationship, leaving you with nothing.

Usually the most effective way to fix your spouse is to fix yourself and wait patiently for a response.

All humans have an almost infinite ability to lie to themselves. We do this for many reasons but primarily to avoid having to accept and forgive ourselves from our past decisions and to avoid having to accept the weaknesses we currently have.

Give permission to your spouse and close friends to point out these lies and then listen carefully to what they share with you. It is

impossible to grow into a better
spouse, a better parent, and a
better person without learning to
come to terms with where you are
right now. However if you do, and
you learn to depend on your
family, good friends, and the
Lord, it will be impossible for you
not to grow. With this growth
will come increased joy, peace,
and happiness for yourself and for
your family.

If you are not comfortable sharing a checking account with your spouse, there is a problem that needs to be uncovered and addressed.

Husband

The kind of leadership a husband is called upon to provide is servant leadership.

Make all major purchase decisions together.

Husband

There is a natural tendency for men who were raised by single moms, or strong moms, to confuse the role of their wife with the role of their mother. Learn to break free of your mother's mothering and learn how to make decisions and be a family leader. Do not go overboard and become controlling of your wife – be a husband, not a boss.

Work to enable each other's joy.

Husband

Hold your wife's hand every once in a while, especially if she's feeling stressed.

Keep your spouse in your life.

Love your spouse the way you love God: with all your heart, with all your soul, with all your strength, and with all your mind.

Wisdom for Marriage

The author invites you to
Make a Difference!

If you think that the message in this book will help guide other couples towards a better marriage and help them to be the best parents that they can be, then please help support this message by going online, registering a rating for the book, and then adding a genuine comment.

Your comments will draw other couples to the wisdom they need to make a difference in their own marriage and in the lives of their children.

My sincere hope is that the words on these pages sparked some new thoughts and conversations that will make a positive difference for you and your spouse in the exiting adventure of parenthood.

Thanks,

Ted LaFemina

Made in the USA
Charleston, SC
03 February 2012